THE DIVORCE LAWYER'S TOOLKIT
Your Secret Weapon for Getting Ahead of the Competition

By Marion TD Lewis, Esq.

The Divorce Lawyers Toolkit

Your Secret Weapon for Getting Ahead of the Competition

By Marion TD Lewis

Copyright © 2016 by Marion TD Lewis. All Rights reserved.
Published by Waterfall Press, Inc. New York, New York
No part of this publication may be reproduced, stored in a retrieval system, or transmitted in any form or by any means, electronic, mechanical, photocopying, recording, scanning, or otherwise, except as permitted under Section 107 or 108 of the 1976 United States Copyright Act, without either prior written permission of the Publisher, or authorization through payment of the appropriate per copy fee to the Copyright Clearance Center, Inc. 222 Rosewood Drive, Danvers MA 01923, (978) 750-8400 fax (978) 646-8600, or on the web at www.copyright.com Requests to the Publisher for permission should be sent to contact@divorcesaloon.com Limit of Liability/Disclaimer of Warranty: While the publisher and author have used their best efforts in preparing this book, they make no representations or warranties with respect to the accuracy or completeness of the contents of this book and specifically disclaim any implied warranties of merchantability or fitness for a particular purpose. NO warranty may be created or extended by sales representatives or written sales materials. The advice and strategies contained herein may not be suitable for your situation. The publisher is not engaged in rendering professional services, and you should consult with a professional where appropriate. Any slights against people or organizations are unintentional. Library of Congress Cataloguing in Publication Data:
Lewis, ISBN: Non Fiction *The Divorce Attorney's Toolkit*
Printed in the United States of America
10 9 8 7 6 5 4 3 2 1

DEDICATION

I dedicate this book to every young lawyer who is courageous enough to try to create and manage a law practice

INTRODUCTION

This book is based on blog posts in the *Lawyer to Lawyer* section of the blog *Divorce Saloon International* which I started back in 2006 when I was practicing Divorce and Family Law in New York City. Indeed, you will find a few posts which have been added verbatim to this e-book.

However, the book is more than just a regurgitation of old blog posts. What I have attempted, and what I hope I have succeeded at doing, is to provide practicing lawyers – especially those just starting out like I was not so long ago – with a competitive edge they will need out of the gate. The book is geared to Divorce and Family Law attorneys, in theory. In practice, I would have to admit that all lawyers in all niches could find it useful – especially the new lawyers just starting out without a clue of how to get clients and how to create and run a successful practice.

When I put up my own shingle in NYC back in the day, I had no idea what it took to build a successful practice. Indeed, it was nuts for me to have attempted to do it the way that I did. What can I say? I did not have a book like this I could refer to, so how was I supposed to know that I needed marketing plans and SEO? Well, eventually, I called it quits and left not just the practice, but the city as well. Eleven years later, sitting in my little studio in Paris, France, this idea for this book came to me. I thought, "why not create a little e-book based loosely on Divorce Saloon – in particular the section *Lawyer to Lawyer* to give young lawyers little tips on how to do this?" Et voilà. Here is the book – *The Divorce Lawyer's Toolkit.* I literally wrote it in two days. Like its sister *The Law School Rules,* which I also wrote in less than one week when I left law school, it is meant to be a quick read you can access on your pc as well as your mobile. (I will create a hard copy version of it as well for those who still like their books in paper format.)

The topics I touched on probably all have some bearing on the things I wish I had known or had done when I had attempted my own solo practice. It was the obvious things, the little things that mattered and still matters – for example, the "contact us" page of your website, or having a marketing plan, or knowing what colors to wear when you go to court, or SEO.

This is the first edition. Hopefully, it will not be the last.

TABLE OF CONTENTS

1. Introduction
2. Your Website
3. Your Online Reputation
4. Your Clients
5. Your Competition
6. The Court
7. Advertising & Marketing
8. Web Marketing Consultants
9. Useful Articles
10. SEO Firms
11. Useful Blogs & Websites
12. Relevant YouTube Channels
13. Credits

1. YOUR WEBSITE

Your website is usually the first contact a potential client will have with you and your law firm. Is it doing its job? Is it optimised? Is it well organized? Is it clear for folks who you are and what your services are? Is it converting clicks into clients? Or is it distracting and self-defeating of your purpose?

A quick troll of the Internet will reveal a lot of different approaches to lawyers' websites. The whole point of having a website is to get traffic and then to convert that traffic into leads and then to convert those leads into paying clients.

The problem is that your website can't do any of that if it is not properly optimised, organized and visible – while at the same time remaining in compliance with the ethical rules for attorney websites (and for this you would defer to your state bar rules as it differs from state to state).

That is the first issue. There is another issue and that is that many lawyers' websites are not as effective as they can be and this is due to very simple, obvious mistakes that they make when creating their sites.

There are many such mistakes. Ten key mistakes lawyers make with their website are identified below. These things are easy to fix and if you pay attention to them when you build and publish your website, you will stay ahead of your competition. Here we go:

1. Be sure to always include your contact details in full. That means that your website should feature a contact us box, display an actual email, and have at least one telephone number visibly displayed on the home page. If possible you should have a toll free number and many lawyers also provide a cell phone number. You should also have your firm address in your contact details as well as links to

any social media pages. A lot of the competition only put a "contact us" box on their website not realising that not all clients react well to the "contact us" box. Some clients are still old fashioned and want to get an email address where they can solicit you from their own private email. Be mindful in the differences among clients' preferences and be sure to have a variety of methods by which they can contact you – not just a "contact us" box.

2. Think about the layout of your home page as well as the formatting, text size and font you use. When it comes to your home page – and really, your whole website – it is all about organization. Don't force your potential clients to have to scroll down too far to get the important information they are seeking on your website because frustration leads to lost clients.

Many lawyers make the mistake of putting the most important details of their services at the bottom of the page; or having text that is too small and therefore difficult to read; or using a font that is aesthetically distracting to potential clients. These things will cause potential clients to click off your site and go to the competition. You should layout your home page using the simple pronouns or adverbs: Who, What, Where, When, How. Use universal fonts like Times Roman – even if they seem boring. This last point is not set in stone, though. Sometimes unusual fonts can stand out and attract eyeballs, this is true. So use your judgment. The key is not to get too crazy with fonts. As for the text size, 14 point font size is probably preferred by some people but 12 points is standard. Anything smaller than 12 though is a mistake. Most people's eyesight just will not accommodate that – especially if you have a lot of text on the page.

3. Think about having a toll free number on the homepage. Clients like to think they are calling you for free.
4. Use video on your homepage to show rather than tell clients how competent and qualified you are to handle their case. It could be a testimonial from another client or a little vignette of you discussing a legal issue. Or, it could be a video involving your firm on the news. Studies show that potential clients appreciate videos. Seeing is believing. The

key with the video though is not to make it too long. A two minute video is all you need. Once you start to get into longer videos clients tune out and click out.

5. Your website should be easy to maneuver and when people click the link should ideally deliver what its name promises. Avoid having too many, if any, dead links on your website. (And btw, with this particular point, do as I say, not as I do.) It's annoying. And watch out for the landing pages

people arrive at when they visit your site from, say, a Google search. In general, your website pages should have simple titles and when the client clicks, the page should correspond to the title and deliver the information promised by the title. Try not to have too many pages on your website that lead to nowhere or that have an error message behind the link. This could be interpreted as unprofessional by potential clients and they could just click away to the next lawyer. Oh, and the pages should be arranged logically. No point putting your "contact us" page at the bottom of your home page in small font. The "about us" should probably be the first page after your home button on the menu. Things like that. Many of the competitors' websites seem to have no rhyme or reason to how the pages are arranged. Do not make this mistake if you want to get ahead of the competition. If you want your website to appeal to your clients and turn clicks into revenues you have to think like the client when arranging your site. My advice? Keep it simple.

6. Use simple vocabulary. Lawyers like to show off their advanced vocabulary and this is great if you are trying to attract and retain other lawyers as clients. But when people are looking for a lawyer, it usually means they are distracted by other problems going on in their lives and the last thing they want to do is decode the vocabulary used on

your website. The choice of words you use should follow this general rule of thumb: if your third grader can understand it, your clients will appreciate it.

7. It is advisable to put your photo on your homepage unless you really feel that your photo will do more harm than good to your credibility. We live in a world where looks do matter a lot, no matter what anyone says to the contrary, and attractive people

definitely have their advantages. But many superb lawyers may not be described as being particularly attractive – and when a client is in a jam, they don't care if you are ugly or cute because they realize that attractiveness does not ipso facto mean competence or expertise. Well, yes and no. For that initial contact, which is the website, some clients *could* look at how you look in determining if they will even call you. So this photo rule is a judgment call. You have to know yourself best of all and make a determination of whether you will put your photo on your website or not. Frankly, if you think your photo will not help to bring in the clients, use stock photos of "potential clients" instead. That is, have a more generic website rather than personalize it to include your photo. This one is totally a judgment call with the ultimate goal being to get the clients in the door.

8. The color scheme of your website matters. It probably is best to have a mostly white or pale background with black text font. But if you have a dark background, you should obviously use white text. A lot of lawyers get very creative with the colors they use on their sites but a lot of it can be very dizzying and very distracting. A soft blue or grey background is good too. Very bright and vibrant colors like yellow, green or red can be overdone and even look unprofessional.

9. Too much information or text on the home page of your website can also be a negative. Leave enough "white space." Do not try to write an encyclopedia on yourself or the law on the home page especially not if it is in infinitesimal text. You want to give just enough information about yourself and your services without going overboard. Leave a little bit for the client to discover when they actually meet you. Too much information is too much

information and worse, it makes your page look cluttered. A cluttered page feels like work to read and most clients don't want to do the work. They get fed up. Instead, they just want a competent lawyer to help them out of a jam, and quick.

10. Many attorneys have a blind side with regard to diversity and how potential clients perceive their firm based on their home page and the website itself. If a client visits an attorney page and sees

only one group of people represented either in the firm or in the stock images the company uses on the site, this could send a message that only certain types of clients are welcomed. Beware of the website that appears to "discriminate" against all but one particular group with respect to its own employees as well as the types of clients it seeks.

11. Finally, be careful not to run afoul of the state ethical rules with respect to being "misleading"

with things like specialization, domain names, truthfulness, content and unauthorized practice of law, etc. With regard to domain names, btw, do spend time selecting the right name for SEO purposes. It doesn't mean you necessarily have to completely rebrand from a dot com to a dot law URL but definitely think about your domain names as this can give you a competitive edge.

2. **YOUR ONLINE PRESENCE**

Clients are going to google you and when they do, they should find an impressive footprint. These days, they are as likely to google you on their home pc as they are on their mobile phone. It behoves you to create, maintain and expand your online presence every chance you get and make sure you look and sound good both on the home pc and on a hand-held device.

Besides having your own firm website, you can do many things to improve your image online. First, you can start a blog. Many lawyers mistakenly think they have to blog just about divorce or whatever area or field of law they happen to be in but this is not necessarily the case. In this day and age, clients understand that their attorneys are multi-dimensional and they appreciate an attorney who has varied interests and is passionate about things other than just their jobs.

So while your blog can be about your work (and arguably, this probably is the best approach) nothing says you can't blog about other topics as well. It could be your hobby such as traveling, food, cars, gardening, sports or any topic that is not on its face inappropriate. You be the judge.

Another way to bolster your online presence is the judicious and strategic use of social media platforms such as Twitter, Facebook, Youtube, Instagram, LinkedIn and their ilk. Again, the important thing is to exercise good judgment when using these platforms, always keeping in mind what your end goal is – to expand your reputation as a lawyer. Is it necessary to subscribe to all social media platforms? No. Obviously, if you are in a position to hire someone to handle your communications for you, then it would be ideal to have a presence on all these platforms – or certainly as many of them as possible. But most lawyers – especially those inclined to read a manual like this – do not have the resources to hire a full time communications director. That means they will be up-keeping their accounts themselves and this can be time consuming. In this case, maybe it is better to choose one platform and do a good job keeping up with it, than to try to have all the platforms and end up not keeping up with any. Which is best if you only have time for one? That will depend on your personality and your personal preferences. The great thing about social media is that there is no dearth of options from which to select.

Another way to boost your online presence is by soliciting client reviews on websites like Avvo and Yelp and other sites that allow clients to rate their attorney and give them stars. This star system seems to be very attractive to clients who, according to research, respond well to lawyers who can garner lots of stars from former clients – the optimal obviously being five stars.

Of course, you will have to take the good with the bad and just like you can get good reviews, you can also get bad reviews. Bad reviews can really be devastating not just to your ego but also to your business. A lot of lawyers have had to file defamation lawsuits against vengeful clients who take to the Internet and with a few clicks on a keyboard destroy what it took 25 years to build. The key here seems to be how you respond to it. The defamation suit is certainly one way but you can also contact the website on which the negative review was published to see if you could negotiate the take down of the review (and you can certainly threaten to sue the website if needed). Barring that you can also respond on the website to the negative review, being careful to remain professional and not to disclose any "attorney/client" privileged information in your response rant lest you should find yourself disbarred for simply defending your good reputation.

And speaking of websites like Avvo, membership in directories and databases is another way to expand your online presence. Again, Avvo, Yelp, Superlawyers, Martindale Hubbell, Findlaw, Lawyers and many others allow you to input your data (often free of charge) and this in turn will expand your visibility online. Divorce Saloon International www.divorcesaloon.com also has a database for lawyers and they are actively seeking members so you should consider that as well.

Yet another way to boost your visibility is to submit relevant articles to websites that solicit them. The Bar Association Journal is an obvious place to start but there are also sites that are not "law" sites that might be worth it as well. There is always Huffington Post, for example, and, of course, Divorce Saloon.

If you have the resources, you can also pay for your online presence by purchasing advertising online. Google's Adwords program is always a good place to start. But you can also buy ads on other people's websites or sponsor websites whose subject matter is relevant but may not be identical to the work you are doing. On Divorce Saloon, for example, we have recently started to solicit "sponsorship" of specific posts on our site. Many other websites have their own specific advertising options and you ought to research the market to see how you can get ahead of your competitors and expand your presence online. Disclaimer: Be careful about the advertising rules in your state. Make sure you don't mess up by breaking any of the rules. Consult the relevant codes before you engage in any advertising campaign.

Making TV and radio appearances – even if not on primetime shows, would be another way of getting your name hooked to a webpage and diffused online, thus expanding your visibility. Indeed with this one, a lawyer who turns down an opportunity to appear on television or on radio to discuss a matter that pertains to their field of expertise is really doing their marketing efforts a great disservice.

Another option for becoming more visible online is to try to get onto lists such as the one we created on Divorce Saloon called the *Titans 10*. With this list we profiled the top divorce lawyers in NYC in 2014 and this page routinely ranks on page one of Google's search results for searches for "best" and "top" divorce lawyer in New York.

Obviously if your name appears on the list, it can only help your marketing efforts. There are many such lists in existence. The idea is to have your name and your firm appear on as many lists of recommended lawyers as possible. This will obviously add to your online creds and clients are likely to think more highly of you when they see your name and your firm on these lists.

Finally, don't overlook the utility of online forums. Many times clients are looking for answers to their questions and the first place they begin is on an online forum. Why not answer some of these questions that are posed, being sure to leave your name and contact details behind?

3. CLIENTS

When it comes to clients, getting and holding on to clients and staying ahead of the competition is not easy especially when clients have so many choices from which to choose. There are a lot of lawyers on every single block and let's face it, many of them are just as competent if not more competent than you –at least so they think. How can you distinguish yourself?

Well, one way is to be the lawyer who is most accessible to clients. Clients complain a lot about their lawyers and one of the main complaints is that their lawyers do not get back to them in timely fashion. Indeed, this is a topic we discussed on *Divorce Saloon.* Read the following post:

Apparently the #1 complaint that clients have about their divorce lawyer is not the exorbitant fees but in fact the slow return of phone calls, text messages and other contact attempts. I am not sure if this is a fair characterization. But if this is the number one complaint, there probably is something to it.

How can divorce lawyers do a better job of quickly returning clients' messages, texts and phone calls? Well, being better organized could help. Having a specific couple of hours in the workday dedicated to returning client calls would be a good idea. Or some lawyers like the idea of just sending a quick response right away so that the client knows you are on the case and that you will re-contact them later when you have more time.

It is true that in this technologically advanced world (how ridiculous this notion will be in 50 years) that clients probably expect a faster turnaround on their calls than is feasible given that the lawyer has to go to court, deal with other clients, conduct research and a whole bunch of other things that make it unreasonable for clients to expect the lawyer to respond right away to every overture.

Having administrative help at the office is obviously a plus so that if you cannot answer at least the secretary can. Not giving out your mobile phone is probably a good idea too. This way the client won't be too angry if you ignore their texts and calls; they will conclude you are probably not at the office and be more content to wait till you get back. But if they have your cell phone, their expectations will change. They will expect you to get back instantaneously.

Another way of managing clients' expectations is to put something in the retainer about how soon you can be reasonably expected to get back to the client. You can have a 48 hour rule in the contract and discuss it during consultation so that the client knows and understands that this can happen. You should also put this rule on your website so it is out there that you can take up to 48 hours to return a phone call. Finally, if all else fails, maybe you just straight up have to try harder to get back to your client right away. This could be the thing that makes your services more attractive than all the other lawyers out there.

Two other ways you can distinguish yourself are your price and the quality of your services. Most attorneys charge roughly the same for their hourly services, on average. But there are some who gouge their clients and others who charge fees that are so low, they threaten the integrity of the whole market. How can you outgun the competition? One way is to offer to have clients set the hourly fee themselves. Yes, of course this sounds insane. Well, you don't have to do it with every client. Only when it seems to make sense. This is a very cutting edge approach and most lawyers would not even consider it, perhaps understandably. This is what makes it attractive to clients, this is what will make you stand out. Imagine when they tell their friends "and he let me name my price I am willing to pay!" In this situation, the client will feel like they are in charge and that they have power, and they will appreciate that. But you obviously have to have some parameters. You can't leave the negotiation so open that the client thinks they can offer you $10 per hour for your services and that this is acceptable. So you offer them alternatives, various different pricing packages. Give them a minimum amount you would accept but contrast it maybe with a fixed fee package that could be just as appealing, and then still negotiate between both options.

What you need to keep in mind is that clients are willing to pay for good services and the attorney that charges the least amount for his or her services is not necessarily the one that the client will pick. There has to be some kind of synergy between the quality of the work they can expect and the price they are being asked to pay for it. But a key consideration when asking clients to set the fee is to always offer an alternative. So you say "you can either set the fee, or we can agree to…but…" Usually, the second option should be very appealing as compared to setting the fee, which, again, should have a minimum price.

To stay ahead of the competition, though, you have to guard against gouging your clients.

This is paramount. Clients are not stupid and they know what the other lawyers are charging. Charging too much is just not good and you can run yourself out of the business especially if the quality of the work does not live up to the price. As we wrote on Divorce Saloon: *"There are divorce lawyers who charge upwards of $700 per hour for a divorce. Is this a fair price for the work involved? When you consider that some online companies are charging a fixed rate of less than*

$500 for the whole procedure from start to finish, how does a lawyer defend an hourly billing rate of $700 per hour? For what are clients paying this much? Seriously? How is this not highway robbery?"

With that all said, we know that the fee you charge is the fee you charge and even if you charge $700 per hour, it is the fee you charge. You are running a business. And your services may be worth it. So this is not a judgment. The question really is how to balance the business aspect of being a lawyer and "making money" with this competing need to help your client save money? It is not an easy thing to circumnavigate. Surely, the competition may not even be mildly concerned about saving the client money. And is it even their job to do that? Is it yours? On *Divorce Saloon*, we wrote the following on the topic: *Divorce lawyers the world over have a bad reputation for being exploitative of their clients' vulnerable state of life and mind. That is to say that, with few exceptions, people see divorce lawyers as greedy sharks who charge usurious fees and who prolong rather than settle divorce cases in order to hit their clients with exorbitant bills at the end of the process.*

This is not an unreasonable charge to level against a significant portion of divorce lawyers. Are we in agreement? But for me, the question is whether it the lawyers' responsibility to save their client money by insisting on settlements when the client wants their pound of flesh, or even to charge at a low hourly rate to suit potential consumers? Or is the responsibility of the divorce lawyer - as a business person - really to their business? Which therefore boils down to them maximizing their economic potential which in turn means racking up as many billable hours as possible?

That is not to say that a divorce lawyer should rack up bogus hours. No lawyer can defend a contemporary who, for example, charges a stay at home mom with a household income under 50K per year 4000 dollars for copies in a divorce action. This shocks the conscience no matter where in the world you live. There is a fine line between understanding and treating your work as a divorce lawyer as a "business" (and trying to make a profit) and completely ripping off a client by charging for bogus expenses; moreover, it clearly is not ethical to advise a client to prolong a case just in order to keep billing. This is clear for everyone.

But the idea is that a law practice is a business; it is not philanthropy. And a divorce law practice is likewise a business - a for profit business. That is, divorce lawyers are in it to make money; to make a profit and that is their first concern. And so what?

I guess the question is whether this is wrong. Should divorce lawyers change their business strategy to make saving their client money a top or, I should say, the *top priority and making a profit their second priority?*

In addition to the price you charge the client, you also need to think about the quality of the services you provide if you want to stay ahead of the competition. Obviously you owe your client a duty of care among others. One of the prime ways in which attorneys fail their clients is with this issue of security and privacy in the digital age. Many lawyers have made critical errors with respect to their digital records and have exposed clients' privacy online. Nothing can ruin a law firm's reputation quicker than having their client's private business exposed online due to their own lapse in judgment with regard to cyberattacks. Cyberattacks and hacks have become easier and easier this is true. But lawyers still have a duty to protect client secrets and thus need to stay on top of all the new technology that will help them to do that. Yes, it is possible to lose clients if you have a reputation for getting hacked and losing clients is obviously not the way to beat the competition.

In this digital age, it is not just about being hacked, however. Keeping clients happy about the quality of the legal services they have received has never been more important. That is because disgruntled, unhappy clients can take to the Internet and destroy your career in less than fifteen minutes. So to stay ahead of the competition, you definitely want to keep client complaints to a minimum. This is the goal. But you have to understand that even after doing your endeavour best for a client, one of them could turn on you unexpectedly. As stated previously, you can definitely respond to some of these online complaints in the most professional manner possible. But in extreme cases where someone obviously is on a vendetta to do harm to your reputation, you may need to get a lawyer yourself to bring an action in tort.

All of this takes time and energy and can be very destructive no matter how it is resolved, sometimes years later. So the best thing is to anticipate problems and try to avoid them from the very start.

A part of that means that you have to carefully select clients. Not everyone who walks into your office waving dollar bills should be given a retainer agreement. It is imperative that a lawyer can read minds and weed out problem clients before they even become clients. See the problem before it actually forms. How can you do this? During the initial interview you need to read the body language. You need to listen to the story the client tells you. You need to even research the client before you accept the case. A client who has had five lawyers for the same case they are trying to retain you on (because the other five lawyers were incompetent) is a problem client. Period. You have to ask yourself: "how badly do I need this $500 bucks?" Because with a problem client, this $500 bucks is not going to be worth it in the end, not after you have to spend a year getting off the case and not after the lasting damage the client will do to you online in negative reviews.

To find good clients is the goal of every lawyer. The good news is that most clients are good clients. They just want some good help and so long as you give them competent legal assistance, they will say thank you and that will be the end of your interaction with them. Or, it might not be. Some clients are so "good," they actually send you clients through referrals. These tend to be the best types of clients. It does not mean you cannot find a bad apple in the midst, who was referred, and yet who turned on you. But usually clients who are referred by other happy clients will also turn out to be good clients.

Where can you find good clients to begin with? A good client is not that hard to find. It is a question of strategy. The first thing to understand is that lawyers who find the most clients are lawyers who are good with people. They understand the importance of networking and being visible in social settings. They join a lot of groups and organizations and they tend to do a lot of volunteering as well as take on leadership roles in these organizations. For example they may join political associations, expat community groups and non-profit organizations. Where possible they try to get on the board of directors or leadership of these groups. It is all about visibility. They may join the coop board in their own building. They are members of their children's school board, as well committees in their churches or synagogues or mosques or what have you. They write for publications geared to specific target groups such as teachers, police officers, doctors & medical professionals and civil servants. They even join interesting meet-up groups. These competitive creatures also advertise in various outlets including using Google Adwords, in trade magazines and on complimentary websites.

Other ways the competition gets good clients is they hire law firm marketing firms to help them market their services effectively to these good clients. There are many law firm marketing consultants who can easily be found on the web.

We have listed a few of them at the end of this book. If you have the budget, there almost is no limit of what they can help you do to promote your law firm. For example, they can provide training for both you and your law firm personnel on various aspects of your practice including how to get and develop business; they can act as your firm's public relations spokesperson – both in good times and trouble times; assist you with creating and distributing newsletters and other promotional items such as email campaigns and e-books; help you with planning and executing and managing "image campaigns" (treat yourself like a brand, like Taylor Swift and get professional help with developing and sustaining your "image"!); assist with conducting market research to see what trends out there could help you tap untapped markets; and otherwise help you with planning and achieving your advertising goals and objectives.

OK. So now that you have found the client and have done a good job for him or her, there are things you can do to keep your clients happy. You can, for example, keep a record of their birthdays and anniversaries and their kids birthdays and send a little card or text to say "happy" birthday or what have you.

You can also throw an annual "thank you" party for former clients. On *Divorce Saloon* we did a post on this topic based on an article we read in

Family Law Magazine

http://familylawyermagazine.com/articles/7-tips-to-maximize-your-summer-marketing :

So I was reading Family Law Magazine *and there was this one article about marketing for Family lawyers. One of the tips was for lawyers to throw a party for former clients to show appreciation for their business and to make it kid friendly if possible so the clients could bring their kids. So you can throw party at the office but you can also have a barbecue at your home in the backyard (could have its risks) or at the local park, at a hotel, a public space or wherever.*

The key is not to make it too complicated so that you can spend quality time chatting up clients and hopefully succeed at not only showing how much you appreciated their business but also drum up new business as well. Obviously you will not get new business from every attendee but depending on the situation, even one new client out of the event could be worthwhile. And no, it does not make you a bad person to have an ulterior motive to your act of appreciation. It just makes you business savvy. So do it. Throw a summer appreciation party for your former clients. Do it within the next couple of weeks!

There are many other things you can do to attract and retain clients in your client database (remember that you have to have one of these). Sometimes you have to be willing to act as a friend or even a mentor to your clients – even when they are no longer active clients. Additionally, while you are not and should not be expected to act as your client's psychiatrist, do not be surprised if clients tend to lean on you from time to time as the burden of their divorce gets overwhelming. Obviously, if this is a situation where you think the client would benefit from some professional help, it is wise to tell the client as gently as possible that they should get that help. Usually though it is not that serious and just a few empathetic words from you could go a long way. Indeed, there are many in the lay population who feel that lawyers in general and not very empathetic. So another way to stand out from your competition is to be more empathetic or to have the reputation of being more empathetic than the next guy

or gal.

4. THE COMPETITION

The competition among lawyers is *fierce*. The main reason is that there is an overabundance of good, competent lawyers in just about every jurisdiction in the country. This phenomenon quite possibly is global. "There are too many lawyers" is a common lamentation no matter where you go in the entire world over.

As if that is not bad enough, divorce lawyers also have to compete with online websites offering bundled divorce services (uncontested divorces in particular) as well as paralegals and paper mills who fill out paperwork for a fraction of the cost of hiring a lawyer on retainer.

It is not always about who works the longest hours. The key seems to be who can optimise their hours of work and get the most out of their day. It is about working smart, not working hard. And again, while you are working smart you have to remember that you have to remain visible to clients. Thus, it is very important to use all your options optimally – including your digital options. Be sure, for example, to fully complete all profiles you "claim" online; make best use of programs like Google places; provide full contact details on your website and on other online platforms; have good landing pages to your sites, etc. This way you can hook the maximum number of leads and potentially convert them into revenues.

The competition can make life difficult in all sorts of creative ways. One is by being uncooperative with requests for documents or adjournments or just keeping their clients under control. This can not only frustrate, it can make you look bad or "weak" to your client and to the court. There are the proverbial opposing counsels from hell and dealing with them effectively can make a difference in how your own client perceives you. If the client thinks that the other lawyer is out-performing you, this could mean trouble not just with that particular client but with potential future clients. The client could literally dissuade people from patronizing your services just because they found you were "weak" when dealing with opposing counsel on their case. So one way to beat the competition is to be assertive. If it is not in your nature to exude assertiveness on cue, learn to fake it till you really *are* it. Or outsource your courtroom appearances and interactions.

One way to beat the competition is just to know more law than they do. Attending CLEs even when you are not due to renew your bar membership is a good idea – and consider CLEs in international venues if you can afford it. There are many international family law associations in the field of Family and Matrimonial law and they have relevant CLEs all over the world. CLEs specific to Divorce and Family law is obviously the best but do not neglect to take other related courses as well if you have the time, resources and inclination. Because this can give you creative ideas and help you take an out-of-the-box approach to your own niche practice and the positive results you potentially reap could be surprising.

There is one particularly troublesome wart about "the competition." It is the issue of "copying." Nobody likes an idea until they see someone else successfully implement that idea. How do you prevent your competitors from stealing your ideas and stealing your clients? This is not easy. Some copying is probably unavoidable. But read articles like the following to get some pointers on how to reduce the copying problem:

How to Stay Ahead of the Competition and Copycats http://nathalielussier.com/blog/online-business-ideas/how-to-stay-ahead-of-competition

and

How to Stand out From You're your Competitors

http://www.thenationaltriallawyers.org/2014/04/how-to-stand-out-from-your-competition/

Don't let your competitors have all the fun at your expense, though. Sometimes you can even turn the tables on them. Read:

7 Ways to Use Your Competitors to Your Advantage for SEO:

http://www.forbes.com/sites/jaysondemers/2016/02/15/7-ways-to-use-your-competitors-to-your-advantage-for-seo/#1a0693606b19

Ironically, as much as you want to outpace your competition, you also would be smart if you are able to work *with* the competition and even team up with them from time to time. That means for example, joining lawyer referral groups where you refer clients to each other as needed. So try not to burn all your bridges.

5. THE COURT

How a lawyer and his or her firm is perceived by judges is very important to their reputation at the courthouse and this in turn affects how they are viewed in the profession and by the community in which they practice. This is not a big newsflash. Except, if you are just starting out. In which case, watch out for the judge, the courthouse and opposing counsel! If you are going to go to the courthouse a lot, you had better be able to elicit respect from the judge and courtroom personnel, and to stand up to opposing counsel without losing your cool.

Divorce and family law judges are not very numerous in most towns. That means that all the judges tend to know the regulars. And all the regulars know all the other regulars. It is a small world and everybody remembers everything. If you are not an insider, you can't be competitive.

One important aspect of your courtroom reputation will be the quality of your submissions to the court and to opposing counsel. Many lawyers take great care to properly edit their work and to present work that is clean, well-organized and professional-looking. Not all lawyers may give as much attention to details, however – and you would be surprised to learn that even seasoned lawyers who have been practicing for many years are guilty of this transgression. This is a mistake. You cannot maintain a competitive edge if you are not paying attention to details like this. The reputation you build in the eyes of the court and your competitors will come down to your attention to the details. Little things do matter to the court, such as the "look" of your motions and your briefs. You really want to be better than the competition in this regard. You want to present your very best.

Of course, it is not just a question of your written submissions. The way you carry yourself as far as your physical appearance in the court room will have some bearing on the way you are perceived by the court. First, you have to pay attention to your body language. Project confidence, authority, self-control and respect. This should not be rocket science but it is a point that seems to escape a lot of lawyers. Second, pay attention to how you cover your body. While it may not be necessary to wear designer suits and cufflinks in the courtroom, doing so will not hurt your reputation or your image. On the contrary, appearing in jeans and sneakers in the court room sends a certain message about how you interpret the court and your place in the process, and your clients. Again, pay attention to details. Think even of the colors in which you are attired, your makeup, perfume, cologne and accessories. Better dressed equals a greater level of success. Luckily, it is never too late to change or tweak this aspect of your brand. Oh, and don't think this is a problem only for one gender. Both male and female lawyers can gain a competitive edge if they simply paid attention to their image and how they "look" to observers such as clients, judges and opposing counsels.

Check out these websites where you can find experts to help you with making over your image. It could be just the competitive edge you need.

1) http://manhattanmakeovers.com/lawyer_image.html

2) http://www.susanbigsby.com/clients.htm

3) http://executive-image-consulting.com/

6. ADVERTISING & MARKETING

There are a number of ways you can distinguish yourself from the competition and get an edge in the field. But it probably is going to mean that you need to, first of all, draft a marketing plan to properly market your firm. Yes, it can be tedious; but you've got to do it. Your goal is to do your best by pre-planning how you will market your firm; and hopefully your plan will be a better, more effective one than the competitor has done with their plan – thus giving you the competitive edge. A better plan means better results, higher revenues, higher level of personal & job satisfaction.

Your marketing plan should include as many methods of marketing your firm as possible. You should consult a marketing expert if you have the resources because this is what they do and they are experts. Methods of marketing a law practice can include using email marketing, social media, Google Adwords, newsletters, branding, etc. Even if you cannot afford a marketing expert there is a lot you can figure out for yourself if you are willing to put in the time. There are countless ways to market a firm successfully and it takes only a few hours of research online to find a fraction of these sources. At the end of this book we have tried to provide you with some places to start. Don't forget, however, that good old word of mouth is probably one of the best ways to market a law practice – or any business for that matter.

The key to effective marketing – and thus your competitive edge - seems to be having a plan for getting a "steady stream of high quality leads" from the get go. You cannot approach marketing your law practice haphazardly. It has to be carefully planned out from the start. Getting leads often means having to create the opportunity for yourself. For this reason, it makes sense to create a client database where you keep track of all your clients and you keep in touch with them so that you can literally *create* your own leads through them, over time.

Once you have your marketing plan, consider how the following items impact not just your plan but your bottom line; and figure out how you can improve or expand on each of them (and note that this is not an exhaustive list):

1. Your website
2. Your brand image/trademark/logo
3. Your Blog(s)
4. Your letterhead & Stationery
5. Your ads such as Google adwords, Facebook ads,

6. Your social media campaign
7. Your PR firm and media representatives
8. Your videos and webinars
9. Your SEO guru
10. Your client database
11. Your law firm newsletter
12. Your Free giveaways and prizes
13. Your e-books and other publications

WEB MARKETING CONSULTANTS WHO CAN HELP YOU

1) Larry Bodine http://www.larrybodine.com/home
2) Jay Pinkert http://www.shatterbox.biz
3) Sue Remley www.jaffepr.com/our-team/sue-remley
4) Thomas E Kane http://www.legalmarketingblog.com/about/
5) Art Italo http://italoconsulting.com/about/
6) Kim Tasso http://www.kimtasso.com/
7) Elizabeth Ferris http://www.ferrisconsult.com/about/
8) Bob Weiss http://www.themarketinggurus.com/
9) Jennifer M. Iverson http://www.firmevolution.com/partners
10) Sue Bramall http://www.bernersmarketing.co.uk/team.html

11) Ed Poll
http://www.lawbiz.com/contact_lawbiz.html
12) Stephen Fairley
http://www.therainmakerblog.com/about/
13) M. Stratford http://lawyermarketingexpert.com/
14) Greg Wildman
http://www.ovclawyermarketing.com/lawyer-marketing-team/greg-wildman
15) Jay Rosenthal
https://www.linkedin.com/in/webattorneymarketing

USEFUL ARTICLES YOU SHOULD READ

1) 6 Tried and True Tips to Attract and Keep your Ideal Clients
   http://www.therainmakerblog.com/2016/08/articles/law-firm-development/6-tried-and-true-tips-to-attract-and-keep-your-ideal-clients/
2) Things I wish I knew starting out in Family Law
   http://www.americanbar.org/groups/young_lawyers/publications/the_101_201_practice_series/things_i_wish_i_knew_starting_out_in_family_law.html
3) Managing your Reputation in an Online World
   http://www.americanbar.org/publications/law_practice_magazine/2014/july-august/simple-steps.html
4) 7 Tips to Maximize Your Summer Marketing
   http://familylawyermagazine.com/articles/7-tips-to-maximize-your-summer-marketing

5) Drawing Customers to your law practice
   http://familylawyermagazine.com/articles/drawing-customers-law-practice
6) 6 Thoughts on Content Marketing Strategy for Law Firms
   http://www.forbes.com/sites/steveolenski/2015/11/26/6-thoughts-on-content-marketing-strategy-for-law-firms/#6fe2760d3d44
7) Best Law Firm Website Designs
   http://www.visualswirl.com/inspiration/best-law-firm-website-designs/
8) 21 Inbound Marketing Strategies to You're your Law Firm
   http://www.natlawreview.com/article/21-inbound-marketing-strategies-to-grow-your-law-firm#sthash.b79fUB15.dpuf
9) 50 Simple Ways to Market Your Practice
   http://www.abajournal.com/magazine/article/50_simple_ways_you_can_market_your_practice

10) 7 Tips For Your Online Lawyer Bio
http://blogs.findlaw.com/strategist/2015/11/7-tips-for-your-online-lawyer-bio.html
11) 5 Online Reputation Management Tips For Lawyers http://www.mycase.com/blog/2015/07/5-online-reputation-management-tips-for-lawyers/
12) Law Firms Now Spending 3.4 percent on Marketing
http://www.lawpracticeadvisor.com/law-firm-marketing-spending/
13) Unholy Law Trinity 3 Ways that Law Firms Suck
http://www.lawfuel.com/blog/unholy-law-trinity-3-ways-law-firms-suck/
14) 4 Ways to Win More Clients
http://www.therainmakerblog.com/2016/07/articles/lead-conversion/4-ways-to-win-more-clients/
15) Rank for Your Name: Reputation Management for Lawyers – and Anyone Whose Name IS Their

Brand http://www.bruceclay.com/blog/online-reputation-management-lawyers/
16) Amazing Facts You Didn't Know that Drive Traffic to Legal Websites http://solopracticeuniversity.com/2015/10/27/amaze-ing-facts-you-didnt-know-that-drive-traffic-to-legal-websites/
17) How to Start Investing in Content Marketing for Small Business http://www.forbes.com/sites/sujanpatel/2015/11/04/how-to-start-investing-in-content-marketing-for-small-business/#4e307da070ba
18) 30 SEO Interview Questions You Must Ask a Prospective SEO Analyst http://www.bruceclay.com/blog/seo-interview-questions/
19) Set Your Traffic on Fire: Latest Ways to Amplify SEO, Including Employee Advocacy – #SMX

http://www.bruceclay.com/blog/amplify-seo-employee-advocacy/
20) Sink or Swim How to Adapt to the New Legal Consumer http://go.avvo.com/new-legal-consumer-download?utm_source=newlegalconsumer&utm_medium=native&utm_content=whitepaper&utm_campaign=sink-or-swim-how-to-adapt-to-the-new-legal-consumer&_ga=1.178695584.526495691.1469881044
21) 4 Tips to Becoming an effective divorce attorney http://soloincolo.com/four-tips-to-becoming-an-effective-divorce-attorney
22) Law Firm Marketing: 9 Tips for Winning More Clients With PPC http://www.wordstream.com/blog/ws/2015/06/29/law-firm-marketing

23) Use Facebook to Boost Your Law Firm's Marketing Strategy
http://blog.legalsolutions.thomsonreuters.com/practice-management-2/use-facebook-to-boost-your-law-firms-marketing-strategy/
24) The Magic of Facebook Ads For Lawyers
http://www.lawpracticeadvisor.com/magic-facebook/
25) Marketing Plans
http://www.forbes.com/sites/davelavinsky/2013/09/30/marketing-plan-template-exactly-what-to-include/#79dfc7b33b82
26) Sample Marketing plans for lawyers
http://www.legalexpertconnections.com/wp-content/uploads/2014/06/Attorney_Marketing_Plan.pdf
27) Attorney Marketing plans
http://www.mplans.com/law_firm_marketing_plan/marketing_strategy_fc.php

28) Why So Many Lawyer Advertising Fails
http://www.writewaysolutions.com/blog/1798/why-so-much-lawyer-advertising-fails/
29) SEO for attorneys
http://webris.org/complete-guide-to-seo-for-lawyers-attorneys/

SEO FIRMS THAT YOU CAN CHECK OUT

1) Juris Digital https://jurisdigital.com/
2) Lawyer SEO https://lawyersseo.com
3) Inside Market Strategy http://www.valleylawyermarketing.com/
4) Black Fin https://goblackfin.com/about/
5) Jurispage https://jurispage.com/2013/seo/law-firm-seo-getting-to-the-top-of-google-search-results-for-your-law-firm/
6) Bruce Clay http://www.bruceclay.com/blog/seo-for-lawyers/
7) PaperStreet https://www.paperstreet.com/seo-results/
8) Rocket Clicks http://www.rocketclicks.com/
9) Radix http://lawfirmseoco.com/
10) Consult Web https://www.consultwebs.com/
11) Webpage FX http://www.webpagefx.com/

12) Amicus Creative Services
 http://amicuscreative.com/
13) Internet Lava
 http://www.internetlava.com/AttorneyLawyer/LawFirmMarketing/FamilyLawDivorce.aspx
14) Ranking coach https://www.rankingcoach.com/fr-fr?gclid=CNWNxsuVoc4CFY4V0wodS-UDlw
15) Stem Legal http://www.stemlegal.com/
16) Ignite Visibility https://ignitevisibility.com/
17) SEO for Lawyers https://www.seo-for-lawyers.com/
18) Think Big Sites http://www.thinkbigsites.com/
19) Edge International http://www.edge.ai/
20) Strategy Consulting
 http://legalresearchmarketingpro.com/consulting-services/
21) Boostability https://www.boostability.com/online-marketing-company/about-us/

22) Digital Current
    http://www.digitalcurrent.com/lp2.html
23) Straight North
    https://www.straightnorth.com/services/seo/?mm_campaign=FD0F0030930A1C173F38B3D35C968A08&mm_replace=true&sncid=2&utm_source=clutch&utm_medium=referral
24) Directive Consulting
    https://directiveconsulting.com/
25) Foxtail Marketing https://foxtailmarketing.com/
26) 180 Fusion https://www.180fusion.com/
27) Lead to Conversion https://leadtoconversion.com/

USEFUL BLOGS & WEBSITES

1) Google plus local http://plus.google.com
2) Google places www.google.com/places
3) Google business www.google.com/business
4) Divorce Saloon www.divorcesaloon.com
5) Avvo www.Avvo.com
6) Mention https://mention.com/en/
7) Viivo https://viivo.com/
8) Ted Walker http://www.talkwalker.com/en/social-media-intelligence/
9) Yelp www.yelp.com
10) EM Advertising http://emcadvertising.com/
11) Get Five Stars https://www.getfivestars.com/
12) One 400 http://one-400.com/
13) Sookasa https://www.sookasa.com/
14) Findlaw www.findlaw.com
15) Superlawyers www.superlawyers.com

16) Martindale Hubbell www.martindale.com
17) Corcoran Law Biz
    http://www.corcoranlawbizblog.com/
18) Meeting Wizard http://www.meetingwizard.com/
19) LinkedIn www.linkedIn.com
20) Justia www.justia.com/lawyers
21) Lawyers www.lawyers.com
22) Attorney Rankings
    https://www.attorneyrankings.org/best-free-law-firm-directories/
23) Nolo http://www.nolo.com/lawyers
24) Facebook www.facebook.com
25) LinkedIn www.linkedIn.com
26) Youtube www.youtube.com

INTERESTING YOUTUBE CHANNELS

1) Book of Business : Realities of Law Firm Rainmaking Book of
   https://www.youtube.com/watch?v=qK0Y3FiUuJw
2) Law Firm as a Business
   https://www.youtube.com/watch?v=P_J8pUvRd_Y
3) CLE MicroSeminar: Legal Ethics of Attorney Websites
   https://www.youtube.com/watch?v=cMvVIz1Amns
4) Law Firm Website Templates-Law Firm Website Design [Get A 100% FREE Law

Website]https://www.youtube.com/watch?v=k0jNqhvMJwU
5) Pay Per Click for Attorneys | Search Engine Marketing | Attorney Websites
https://www.youtube.com/watch?v=taYtJUON0KQ
6) Legal Marketing Fort Lauderdale | Ft Lauderdale Law Firm Marketing-For A Steady Flow Of New Clients
https://www.youtube.com/watch?v=srZyFoiFVuo
7) How to Make Social Media Work your your Law Firm
https://www.youtube.com/watch?v=SyU91XBdt_8
8) 8 Things Killing Your Law firm and How to Stop Them
https://www.youtube.com/watch?v=AfC1vmd1CDA
9) Attorney Internet Marketing | How to Acquire 10+ Clients Each Month!

https://www.youtube.com/watch?v=BnLuPMaSgUA
10) Martindale-Hubbell Competitive Essentials for Law Firms
https://www.youtube.com/watch?v=xxztGh_MWCw
11) Courtroom Etiquette
https://www.youtube.com/watch?v=4lPnG1HMkBg
12) Introduction to the AAML Best Practices Video Series
https://www.youtube.com/watch?v=RNLHfWulzSw

CREDIT

Cover photograph courtesy of Flickr Creative Commons https://www.flickr.com/photos/ann-dabney/3509093544/in/photolist-6m62fQ-nUG2mr-oG4rWr-ogdxvg-4FYzNA-oguXFT-6su5Va-bo4TaL-m1aJ5-d9WKhE-5d9s7f-5oy5Vk-bAYJLP-oRFskV-8SPw4f-6gnLn2-51X7iC-4UoExP-7GqtqJ-duu1vN-2Hoop-gsZosi-51Wm9S-5UHWHw-dNhqvt-gS3mA-4GPdwV-4Ykwv4-4GPdBt-4GTow1-4ZiCY4-5t7CyN-8UosBX-4GTowW-awUbFk-4HYq6b-5cz5G6-753vLH-5pPwxu-4Ns5LQ-nrvVpH-f9gHFx-7o1h9X-5CAc6Q-rfz2WT-c6bmEy-6cZtvw-ooYEYx-6aZfin-4MbyGo

STAY TUNED FOR THE NEXT EDITION

www.ingramcontent.com/pod-product-compliance
Lightning Source LLC
Chambersburg PA
CBHW070257190526
45169CB00001B/440

www.ingramcontent.com/pod-product-compliance
Lightning Source LLC
Chambersburg PA
CBHW070257190526
45169CB00001B/440